MW01095087

# SHE CREATES THE WAY

# SHE CREATES THE WAY

Ditch the Traditional 9–5,
Rock Your Side Hustle, and
Pave Your Path as a Female Entrepreneur

By Jessica DeBry

# SHE CREATES THE WAY

www.shecreatestheway.com

Jessica DeBry

Cover Design by Miladinka Milic at
www.milagraphicartist.com

This book is dedicated to my mom, dad, and sister.
Thank you for always believing in me.
I am forever grateful for your love and support.

## FREE BONUS BUNDLE

Access printable PDFs, inspirational wallpapers, & more!

**To download go to: www.shecreatestheway.com**

# TABLE OF CONTENTS

she is
fearless,
determined,
& unstoppable.
she creates the way.

# INTRODUCTION

## welcome

If you're feeling stuck and stagnant with your current reality, you're not alone.

I connect with women nearly daily who all say the same thing. They are yearning for more. More money, more freedom, more time, more purpose, and more excitement in their every day.

They all have one thing in common: a burning desire to ditch the traditional path and carve their own way in entrepreneurship.

If you're ready to stop dreaming and start doing, this book is for you.

Perhaps you worry that you don't have the mindset, tools, or time to make it happen. I'm here to prove to you that that is absolutely false.

You don't need to be perfectly ready with a large bank account as backup to make your entrepreneurial dreams come to life. You simply need the desire and spark to jumpstart your journey.

I wrote this book for every woman that has been in my shoes, feeling lost in the 9–5 world and searching for a way out. Wanting to just up and quit but faced with the reality that I needed to stick around and collect a paycheck, I chose the alternate path: side hustle.

By building your business on the side (while still juggling your 9–5 job), you set yourself up for a future lifestyle business that is better than your wildest imagination. Because when you learn to monetize and grow on your already short time constraints, by the time you quit corporate and become a full-time entrepreneur, you've created a freedom-based business that is more fulfilling and financially rewarding than any 9–5 job could be.

*She Creates the Way* is designed not only to teach you the three crucial components to transform your side hustle into solopreneur success, but also to inspire your adventure into entrepreneurship with seven important life lessons necessary for paving your own path.

As a business owner who had no choice but to take the side hustle route after my first entrepreneurial endeavor failed, I've spent thousands of dollars and countless hours learning and growing from my previous mistakes.

I spent fifteen months side hustling with my online business while still working full time, determined to finally make my dreams of business success come to fruition.

Now, I'm truly living my dream. As I type this, I'm sitting in a cafe overlooking the Pacific Ocean, on a quick random trip out to Newport Coast, California. It's 11:04 a.m. on a Tuesday, and as I sip my almond milk latte and watch the palm trees sway in the breeze, I am overwhelmed with gratitude for where this path has taken me.

While my own side hustle focused on coaching and consulting, shortly after I left corporate, I launched a subscription box designed for female entrepreneurs who are also building their business on the side. SHEclub Monthly has been a massive success from the start, and we've sent out thousands of boxes to women who are following their visions of business ownership.

The truth is, entrepreneurship is scary. You don't have a steady paycheck and you're following a future based on a dream.

But your entrepreneurial dream doesn't need to remain a fantasy. I'm living proof that you CAN make it a reality, and *She Creates the Way* will help you get there.

I promise that if you follow the lessons and advice presented in this book, you'll be prepared to claim your destiny as a successful female entrepreneur.

In Part One, we'll dive into the seven crucial life lessons necessary for paving your path in entreprencurship. This is the mental foundation to the right mindset that is so often overlooked on the journey, yet it is undeniably important in shaping our actions.

In Part Two, we'll talk about practical steps for starting and growing your business. You'll learn the three crucial components to transform your side hustle into solopreneur success, and how to get back to the basics with ten steps to online business prosperity.

Throughout this book, you'll read real-world stories of women (just like you) who have created their own path—and how they got there.

Don't be the gal who thinks about her big dreams and simply says, "Someday, when the stars align . . ."

The truth is, there has never been a better time to take what you're passionate about and build a business around it.

Now is your time to take action and turn your big scary goals of entrepreneurship into reality.

It's time to say buh-bye to a lackluster existence and carve your own path. It's time that *She Creates the Way.*

# PART ONE

## embrace life's lessons

# CHAPTER 1

# follow the nudges

I was beginning to think that I'd lost my mind.

I should have felt excited and fulfilled.

After all, just one month prior, I started working at my dream job.

I'd been hired as a marketing communications specialist in a growing coaching company and knew from the moment I went in for the interview that I wanted the job.

There was a buzz of enthusiasm around the office. The sales teams were smiling while making sales calls (and a football was being hurled from one corner to the other). The customer service reps were settling into their cubicles after filling their coffee mugs from the fancy single-brewed coffee machine in the break room. And the digital marketing team (my soon-to-be coworkers) were huddled around a floor-to-ceiling whiteboard, analyzing numbers from a recent live event.

After I left my first interview, I smiled the entire drive home. When a few days passed and I got the call with a job offer, I had one of those scenes from the movies where the main character throws her hands up in the air, runs to the bedroom in a fit of laughter, and jumps up and down on the bed with a huge grin on her face.

I was overjoyed to get the job.

So why, only one month later, was I feeling unsatisfied and unfulfilled?

Why was I waking up with an unsettled feeling in the pit of my stomach?

*What the heck was the matter with me?!?*

I thought maybe I was going through a little bit of a funk.

One Tuesday night, after arriving home from work, I put dinner on the stove and poured myself a glass of chardonnay (and put on comfy clothes and slippers, of course), then called up my best friend, Christie, to ask her if she thought I was going crazy.

"It's just a phase," she advised. "You just started! Give yourself time to settle in. You're probably just overwhelmed or something. You'll get over it."

"I hope so." I sighed.

"You're doing everything right," she assured. "This is part of your path!"

Argh. *The path.*

The traditional path.

It's what we're told to follow to make all our dreams come true.

Get good grades. Get accepted into college. Study hard. Graduate with a degree. Start working for a growing company. Dedicate yourself to your job. Climb the corporate ladder. Live happily ever after.

But what happens when the traditional path doesn't lead to happiness? And instead of feeling fulfilled with your path, you're left lost and confused?

This is where I found myself after taking all the "right steps" on the traditional path.

A bachelor's degree, an MBA, years dedicated to corporate America, and a new gig that was supposed to be my dream job.

I had taken all the right steps, yet I felt in my heart that perhaps the traditional path wasn't for me.

It was a scary thought to consider . . . to entertain the idea that everything you know may be wrong.

However, what you know logically is very different than what you feel in your heart.

*And you have to listen to your heart.*

Here's the thing about life: there's no instruction manual. There's no step-by-step breakdown of exactly what you need to do (like when you purchased that bookcase from IKEA and opened up the box to thirteen sheets of plywood and a forty-seven-page step-by-step assembly instruction list).

So we default to what we know. We do what logically makes sense.

Somewhere along the lines, we feel a twinge in our heart.

A pull in our soul.

A nudge, if you will.

These nudges don't outright tell us what to do. But they help us ponder beyond the current situation that we're in, and they appear in many different forms . . .

A feeling in the pit of your stomach. A relentless daydream. And in my case, a slight feeling of dissatisfaction, even though all was perfect from the outside.

*Follow the nudges.*

The nudges are your compass, guiding you to where you really need to go.

At this point, I knew that I had two options . . .

Option A: Ignore the twinges of dissatisfaction and continue along the traditional path. Dedicate myself to a company.

Work my way up. Score a corner office and a 2 percent raise every year. And all the while *feel completely unfulfilled with my work and life.*

Option B: Follow the nudges. Dig deep into what lights me up. Pursue my passions. Face the unknown. Figure it out as I go. Feel utterly terrified and unbelievably excited all at the same time.

Given the two options, I realized there really was only ONE option (hint: it wasn't Option A!).

And slowly, while still working full time, I pursued passion projects and entrepreneurial endeavors on the side.

Fifteen months later, I quit my "dream job," said goodbye to the traditional path, and realized that happiness isn't created in the mind . . .

Happiness comes when you listen to your heart and follow your nudges.

> You can't connect the dots looking forward; you can only connect them looking backwards. So you have to trust that the dots will somehow connect in your future. You have to trust in something—your gut, destiny, life, karma, whatever. This approach has never let me down, and it has made all the difference in my life.
> —Steve Jobs

Right now, at this exact moment in your life, you're feeling a nudge . . . an ever-so-soft tap on the shoulder that it's time to do something different.

Lean into that feeling. Explore the choices that you can make in order to get closer to what lights you up.

You probably already know what direction you want to take. But you're looking for a sign before you actually choose to take it.

Girl, THIS is your sign.

It's time to make the choice.

And even if you don't know what the pathway looks like, trust in yourself that you'll figure it out as you go.

Choose your path.

Commit to your nudges.

**Embrace the Lesson: Follow the Nudges
[3 Journal Questions]**

Question One: Where in my life have I been feeling dissatisfied?

Question Two: Why is my current reality not currently matching my expectations (and what can I do differently to change this)?

Question Three: What am I being nudged toward? (What am I truly passionate about?)

# CHAPTER 2

## *you are not your past*

Sheila had every reason NOT to have a promising future.

She grew up poor, in a tiny three-bedroom, one-bathroom house, with eight siblings. (Including Sheila and her parents, that's twelve people split between three rooms—not to mention sharing ONE bathroom!)

Food was so scarce in the household that the moment a meal was placed in the middle of the table, the kids would fight and scramble to try to get a portion of food. The entire meal would be gone in minutes.

She went to bed hungry many nights.

And at the tender age of two, with her wispy blonde hair and sparkling blue eyes, Sheila suffered a freak accident . . .

It started as a lighthearted night. The kids found out that *The Wizard of Oz* was being broadcast on the television and were so excited that they started to parade around their tiny living room. They grabbed household objects to hold in their small hands in celebration.

Unfortunately, in the excitement, Sheila's eye was stabbed with a pencil and she suffered permanent vision loss in her left eye.

This tragic accident changed her life forever.

Her family was too poor to afford a proper prosthetic, so she grew up with an ill-fitting glass eye.

Sheila was teased mercilessly in school. She was bullied on a daily basis.

As a young teenager, she fell into a deep depression. She felt that suicide was the only way out.

Late one night, after a particularly hard day, Sheila hit rock bottom. She cut her wrists, not wanting to be forced to endure the incessant teasing.

Fortunately, her suicide attempt was unsuccessful.

Not soon after, her school was able to help her in seeing a therapist to work through her depression.

Slowly but surely, Sheila started to turn things around.

She started to find meaning in her life.

Sheila decided to focus on the future and forget her past.

As the years went on, she hit every goal that she put in front of herself.

As a young twenty-something, she discovered that she loved writing and fitness, and scored a highly coveted position as a writer for *Muscle & Fitness* magazine.

Later, after meeting a cute and smart guy (and soon-to-be husband) while in college, she was inspired by his desire to become a mechanical engineer, so she decided to become one too (even though females in the field were unheard of).

After entering the workforce and starting to make her dent in engineering, she moved to beautiful Orange County, California, and purchased a home that was triple the size of the one she grew up in.

And even while society told her it was impossible to have a lucrative career AND start a family, she became a mother to two ambitious daughters—including the one writing this book. (Yes, Sheila is my mother . . . Love you, Mom!)

Sheila created her own pathway, that was a far cry from her lonely, poor, depressed upbringing.

And she is a perfect reminder of the fact that *your past does not equal your future.*

So many of us get caught up in our past experiences.

We play the same stories over and over in our heads and throw blame as the reason why we can't move forward.

We create our own prisons for ourselves, crafting excuses rooted around our past about why we can't achieve our dreams.

When in reality, every moment is a new opportunity to start over.

Every second is a fresh start.

Your past doesn't matter.

Your past doesn't have to define you.

Most importantly, your past doesn't dictate your future.

Even if you've experienced horrible things or gone through traumatic events, know that your future is a clean slate to create whatever your heart desires.

## A Tale of Two Sisters

Have you heard the old story of the two brothers who grew up in the same circumstances but ended up with very different paths in life? I've adapted it to fit this book (so, hello, sisters!).

Two sisters grew up in the same home, with a single mother.

Their mom was an alcoholic and had several run-ins with the law.

When the two sisters grew into adults, they created two opposite realities.

One sister had a life very similar to her mother's. She suffered from alcoholism and found it difficult to hold down a job. Her marriage fell apart and she lost touch with people she was once close with.

When asked why her life was the way it was, she replied, "How could it not be, given what I grew up in?"

The other sister had a very different life. She opened a local coffee shop and was a prominent figure in her community. She took care of herself and others around her. She had a loving husband and strong relationship with her kids.

When asked why her life was the way it was, she replied, "How could it not be, given what I grew up in?"

Two sisters, with the same past . . . *and two very different outcomes.*

Two sisters, starting in the same place, with the same circumstances. However, they chose completely different paths as a result of their situation.

You can't choose what happens to you . . . but you CAN choose how you respond.

You can't control the circumstances, but you have total and complete control over your reaction.

We all have the power to choose.

Choose to let go.

Choose to move forward. Choose to take hold of the unlimited potential that you KNOW you have within you.

## Embrace the Lesson: You Are Not Your Past
## [3 Steps]

Step One: Identify the Story

What's holding you back? The first step is to look within and identify what part of your past is keeping you from moving forward. This is called a *limiting belief* and is simply a false story! Pinpoint the story and remind yourself that it does not define who you are.

Step Two: Get Present

Now it's time to move into the here and NOW by getting present. My favorite way to get present? I find a spot outside, close my eyes, and open my senses to everything around me . . . the feel of the wind, sound of the trees, smell of the grass, etc. The key here is to take time to focus on exactly what is happening in the moment, therefore tuning out the loud stories of the past.

Step Three: Look Forward

What do goal setting, business planning, creating a vision board, and daydreaming all have in common? They are all future-oriented activities. Now that you've said buh-bye to your silly past story and tuned yourself into the present moment, it's time to keep both eyes on the road ahead. Choose whatever future-oriented activity excites you most (I love creating vision boards!) and run with it. Your future is filled with unlimited possibility!

# She Create[d] The Way

*True stories of women with big dreams, just like you, who have paved their own paths as female entrepreneurs.*

### Kathrin Zenkina

Kathrin Zenkina is the founder and creator of Manifestation Babe. She has built a seven-figure business on teaching women how to manifest their dream lives.

But Kathrin isn't just talking the talk . . . she's walking the walk and knows firsthand how important it is to manifest mentally before manifesting in reality.

When she first launched Manifestation Babe, she was $25,000 in debt, working as a secretary and trying to keep her failing MLM business afloat. Manifestation Babe had made zero money. She felt like she had nothing to show for the insane hard work she'd put into building her business the last two years and wondered where she went wrong. Here's how she tells it in her own words:

> This time of my life was the lowest point I've ever hit. I was scared, frustrated, and couldn't believe how I got myself into this situation
>
> I just moved to Los Angeles to pursue my dream . . . building a business under the palm trees by the beach, and life went completely

the opposite direction for me. I attended a Tony Robbins event, where I signed up for a credit card, charging $15,000 to join a high-level program, having no idea how I was going to pay it back.

I was scared. But I KNEW I had to invest in myself, and I was determined to do anything to be successful. I was making only $400 a week at the time and had no money to afford rent (hence the family couch surfing!), pay off my debt, or even start a decent savings account.

Kathrin was haunted with thoughts that she would never be able to get out of debt. She would lie awake at night, thinking the following:

How will I pay this off?!
How will I increase my income to get out of this hole I'm in?
How will I pay my bills?
Do I even have enough for my next grocery run?
What if I have a money block that's keeping me broke?!
What if I end up homeless?

After doing some journaling one morning, Kathrin realized she'd had a crappy money mindset her entire life. So, she did the work. She ignored the voice in her head and turned on the tunnel vision to her studies.

She studied. She applied. She took fearless action. She kept going. *And it worked.*

Kathrin went from $25,000 in debt making just $400 a week in her direct sales business, to being financially free, having over six figures in savings and investments, and having consistent $80K–$100k months in her own fulfilling business, in just under a year.

Today, Manifestation Babe enjoys $100k+ months and keeps growing exponentially—in a total of just eighteen months since Kathrin made the decision to master money.

> Money is where I see so many women get stuck. They know they want more of it. They know that deep inside they were meant for a life of freedom, luxury, and fulfillment.
>
> But you have to be willing to double down on yourself. To go all in. When that happens . . . everything changes.

# CHAPTER 3

# stare fear in the face

The dreaded indoor cycle bike.

Argh.

That dreaded indoor cycle bike caused a big, embarrassing gym fail for me when I was a teenager, and the incident has haunted me ever since.

Note to self: don't try to adjust a gym machine by yourself that you've never used before.

Note to self, part two: when the seat of your indoor cycle bike (that was adjusted incorrectly) falls off and you go tumbling to the ground in the middle of a packed gym at sixteen years old, just smile and laugh it off. Don't scream. You'll draw more attention to yourself. *Trust me on this one.*

So WHY, all these years later, was I even contemplating trying out an indoor cycling class?

Well, the truth is that I had heard all the rage about "Spin Class".

But the real truth is that I was feeling a little flabby and needed a good kick in the butt to get myself motivated to work out.

So when my local cycling club was offering a free class, I forced myself to sign up.

I had knots in my stomach the morning of the class. The entire drive over to the studio, my mind kept coming up with reasons why I didn't need to go.

I was terrified that this indoor cycle class was going to be the bigger and badder sequel to "Jessica Falls Off Bike and Makes a Big Fool of Herself."

Not to mention, I was terribly out of shape. I hadn't stepped foot in any sort of exercise arena for years.

All of these reasons why I couldn't successfully complete the class kept compounding in my mind.

But I forced myself to go, even amongst my bundle of nerves.

I parked the car and walked into the studio with my head held high. I put on the cycle shoes and made my way into the dimly lit room, where I chose bike number 27, took a deep breath, and mentally told myself to "get through it."

The cycle studio had two large television monitors surrounding the instructor. These monitors would show our class ranks at the end of our fifty-minute ride.

It was then that the competitive streak surged within me. I didn't want to just get through the class . . . I wanted to be in the top 5!

The entire fifty-minutes, I pushed myself. My legs burned as I cycled faster than I ever thought possible. Halfway through, I felt so nauseous and light-headed that I figured there was no way I could make it to the end without either vomiting or passing out.

When the lights came up in the last five minutes indicating the cooldown of the class, I breathed a heavy sigh of relief. "I made it!" I thought to myself.

Then, the class ranks started posting on the big screens . . .

Jessica D, bike #27: 35/35.

Thirty-fifth place . . . out of thirty-five people in the class?!?

Dead last. *Argh.*

You know, normally I would've been a little discouraged of my absolute dead-last ranking, but truthfully, I was proud of myself.

Proud of facing my fear of that dreaded indoor cycle bike, ignoring my inner excuses, and doing something that I was scared to do.

After I walked out of that first indoor cycle class, I was on such a high that I decided to sign up for a month-long unlimited membership.

Over the course of the next thirty days, I would go to twelve cycle classes, questioning my sanity every time I drove to class. I would hit third place on my tenth class, have several occasions where I shed tears, and most importantly, feel absolutely unstoppable each time I walked out of a completed session.

In fact, I credit those cycle classes for giving me the motivational push to write this book, increase the pricing in my one-to-one business coaching, and deciding to host my first in-person event.

Because by overcoming my silly fear of the dreaded indoor cycle bike, I was reminded that fear is just an illusion.

**FEAR = False Evidence Appearing Real**

How many times have you had big goals and dreams for yourself and your business, only for fear to stop you in your tracks?

Maybe it's starting a blog, or selling something you made on Etsy, or creating a business around something you love, or starting a podcast, or whatever else you dream of doing.

But every time you think about it, fear gets in the way, like a big scary man standing at the beginning of the bridge to your big dreams, staring at you deep in your eyes, and yelling, "Thou shalt not pass!"

Fear has become the BFF to resistance . . . and now, it's not even the direct fear you're feeling, it's the resisting pull backward to safety that is holding you back.

You resist working on your blog, or opening up your Etsy account, or writing a business plan, or recording your first podcast episode, etc. . . . all because, deep down, you're afraid.

You're afraid that others will judge you.

You're scared that you'll look stupid.

But most of all, you're terrified that you'll fail.

*Fear is holding you back from stepping into your true potential.*

Here's the thing about it: fear is a LIAR. And there are two very important lies about fear that you need to know . . .

**Two Lies About Fear**

LIE #1: Fear Dissipates Through Proper Planning

If you're trying to plan your way through the fear . . . STOP.

So many of us mistake learning and planning as a form of taking action, when in reality, that's simply just another form of resistance.

Instead of building your business, you just PLAN to build a business.

And then you get caught in the never-ending loop of planning because you're held back by fear.

The truth is, there's only one thing that helps dissipate fear, and that's *taking action.*

It's not the thinking that stops the fear; it's the doing.

So if you find yourself held back by the need to plan, identify this as the perfect opportunity to stop the planning process and move forward to the next step of taking action.

Feel the fear and do it anyway.

LIE #2: Successful People Don't Feel Fear

It's easy to look up at ultra-successful people and imagine that the reason they've been able to achieve so much is because they are fearless.

But the reality is that they feel fear just like the rest of us.

Take Barbra Streisand for example. A singer, songwriter, and true American icon, Streisand is recognized by Billboard as holding the record for the most top-10 albums of any female recording artist.

She also admits to being a long-time sufferer of stage fright.

During a live performance in front of 150,000 people in Central Park in 1967, Streisand fumbled, went blank, and forgot her own lyrics.

Afterward, her fear became so big that she turned down all paid live shows for twenty-seven years . . . nearly three decades!

Streisand continued to make music and sell albums during this time, becoming a self-made millionaire. And twenty-seven years later, she made the conscious choice to face her fear of the stage.

In an interview with ABC News in 1995, when asked how she was able to overcome her fears, Streisand chuckled. "I haven't necessarily overcome it," she said about her pre-stage nervousness. "I have to deal with it. You know what? I don't know many performers who don't have it."

To be human is to feel fear.

The only difference between those who reach success and those who don't? Even though the fear is there, they have the will to push through it, no matter what.

Most importantly, remember that fear is an indicator of change.

And if you're afraid of something, know that the feeling of fear is simply an indication that you are getting closer and closer to your big goals.

Embrace the feeling. Face your fears.

> **Embrace the Lesson: Stare Fear in the Face**
> **[Visualization Prompt]**
>
> Just for a moment, I invite you to close your eyes and participate in a personal visualization. Think to yourself, what would you do if you weren't afraid? What could you accomplish without fear in the way?
>
> Visualize the possibilities of achieving everything you can imagine and removing the fear. Recognize the power that you have within you and know that your will is stronger than your fear.
>
> Mantra to repeat: *My faith is stronger than my fear!*

# CHAPTER 4

## learn as you go

"I can't believe you're leaving me!" my younger sister Diana yelled jokingly with a half-smile.

"Don't worry," I said. "It's only for six months."

"Six months is like a lifetime!" she replied.

We were standing over two large suitcases in my bedroom, trying to stuff in as many items as possible into the already overstuffed bags. In less than twelve hours, I'd be on a plane up to Vancouver, Canada, to join a cruise ship, my new home for the next six months.

I'd been hired to work onboard the Carnival Spirit, a huge three thousand-person cruise ship, as their destination shopping specialist. Having just graduated college only two months prior, the opportunity to travel and get paid for it seemed like a dream come true.

I was excited. But I was also terribly anxious.

I tossed and turned all night, filled with giddy anxiousness about my new journey ahead.

As I said my goodbyes to my family the next morning and hopped in the SuperShuttle to the airport, reality hit me: I didn't really have any idea what I was doing.

I leafed through my onboarding papers, trying to get a better grasp of my new role and the training I'd be undergoing when I joined the ship.

"Dear Jessica," the letter began.

> Congratulations! Welcome aboard.
>
> We're so excited to have you join us as our new destination shopping specialist. Your role is to educate the guests on the best places to shop in our various ports of call.
>
> Destination shopping specialists are responsible for creating a huge shopping frenzy for the ports of call. This is accomplished through convenient office hours and live onboard presentations to upwards of one thousand guests.

I hovered my eyes over that last sentence for a few moments.

One thousand guests?!?

Gulp.

> As the destination shopping specialist, your duties are completely autonomous. You will not have a direct supervisor onboard; however,

you will be required to send a check-in email to the home office at the end of each week.

To get acquainted with your new position, you will have seven full days of onboard shadowing with the current DSS, Justine. Justine will share the current scripts and formats for the live onboard presentations and walk you through all of the required office hours tasks.

Justine will complete her final week as you follow and observe the proper responsibilities of the destination shopping specialist role before you take over.

We're pleased to have you on the Carnival Spirit!

I set the welcome letter down and looked up, just as the shuttle was pulling up to the curb at the airport.

The entire day I spent in airports and airplanes. As I glanced out the small window at thirty-five thousand feet in the air, I reassured myself that it was silly of me to be nervous . . . I mean, Justine was going to teach me everything, right?

Night fell, and I was on my final leg of the journey: a short taxi ride from the airport to the cruise ship.

I hopped onto the curb, lugged my two large suitcases behind me, and stood in front of my new home for the next six months.

The ship was massive. I was intimidated by its size.

"Can I really do this?" I said to myself, feeling the waves of anxiousness come back over me again. I reassured myself that everything would be fine, because Justine would be there.

I didn't really know what I was doing, but I knew Justine would show me what to do. She would walk me through everything I needed to know.

Unfortunately, all of my mental reassurances about Justine came crashing down as soon as I walked onboard and the ship started pulling away from the dock.

"Are you Jessica?" the cruise director asked. "I hope so! Justine had to leave the ship early due to a family emergency. We were worried that we wouldn't have a destination shopping specialist this go-round, so . . ."

"Huh!?" I cut him off. "I mean, yes, I'm Jessica. But where's Justine? She's not here!?!?"

I could feel my lower lip start to tremble as the weight of the situation sunk in.

I was on a strange, large cruise ship, in a new job that I knew nothing about . . . with no one to show me what to do.

Gulp.

"Nope, she's gone . . . but you'll do fine! Heads up that you've got your big onboard presentation in three days. But don't worry, the ship is only at 80 percent capacity, so the turnout to your gig should be closer to 750 guests instead of 1,000," he said.

Big gulp: 750 people?!? In only three days?

In three days, 750 people would get to see me make a complete fool of myself. *Great.*

At this point, I didn't know what I was going to do. In any other situation, I would've left: quit the job, left the scene, and returned back to a place of safety and comfort.

But here, I didn't have that option. I was stranded in the middle of the ocean. LITERALLY.

And unless I wanted to strap on a life vest and steal a tender boat to try to navigate back to shore in the middle of the night, I was going to have to deal with it.

So I accepted my fate and charged ahead.

Over the next three days, I talked to all the crew members who had worked with Justine, asked questions, and soaked up as much knowledge as possible about my new role. I also emailed the home office and was able to gct a partial script for my presentation.

I was still filled with anxiousness, but I told myself that I would do my best.

I would learn as I go.

When the day of the live destination shopping show rolled around, I wasn't ready. But I didn't have a choice. I went up there and completed my presentation, trembling the entire time. (Seriously . . . the AV guy later told me that he thought the mic was malfunctioning because my voice sounded so spotty, ha!)

As the weeks rolled on, I picked up more knowledge and tweaked my approach. And after a rough start, I embraced the role and actually started to enjoy the big live presentations.

Six months later, when my final week onboard the ship arrived, the cruise director approached me with a smile.

"Jessica, I have to tell you, and don't take this the wrong way, but you've really come far from where you started!"

I tilted my head and replied, "What do you mean by that?"

"Well," he continued, "I think we were all a little worried after your first week onboard. You were running around like a chicken with your head cut off! And your first presentation . . . sheesh! Well, let's just say that's long forgotten. You've really learned a lot! I think you've become one of the best destination shopping specialists I've worked with."

I chuckled. "Ha! Well . . . thanks!"

Looking back, the six months I spent working on a cruise ship became so much more than six months of travel and fun. It was in those six months that I learned the advantage of the "learn as you go" approach.

Later, when I eventually left corporate and jumped into entrepreneurship, this lesson proved to be invaluable. Because it stresses the importance of doing and learning instead of thinking and stalling.

Here's the thing about being an entrepreneur that is completely different than being an employee: there's no boss to tell you what to do.

There's no employee handbook to refer to.

There's no list of responsibilities to guide you.

But this is what makes business building so dang interesting (and fulfilling!).

By keeping an open mind and absorbing everything that comes your way, you can shape and shift everything about your future—both yourself and your business.

And if there's one thing you need to remember about the "learn as you go" approach, it's that you don't need to know everything. The only thing you need to know is that you'll learn it as you go along.

In casual terms, this is called "winging it" . . . but let's not downplay the power that comes with jumping in with both feet and figuring out everything as it comes.

You don't need to know how to take the next twenty steps forward; you just need to know how to take the FIRST step. Then you'll learn how to take the next step as you go.

Rest assured that everything you need to know will come to you as you get closer to it.

Trust in yourself. You CAN figure it out. *You got this, girl!*

**Learn as You Go: A Billionaire's Tale**

Sara Blakely is the Founder of Spanx. She's also a billionaire. Yes, billionaire with a *B*!

But before all of the magazine covers, Oprah features, and massive success, Sara was just a woman with a dream living in a small Atlanta apartment.

Spanx began when Sara was getting ready for a party one night and she realized she didn't have the right undergarment to wear under a pair of tight white pants. Using scissors, she cut the feet off her control-top pantyhose. The result was so revolutionary that she knew she had to pursue it as a business!

The thing was, Sara knew absolutely nothing about building a business. She was clueless of the women's undergarment industry, patenting a new product, manufacturing, marketing, product development, website development, online commerce, etc.

But she KNEW she could figure it out.

Sara is the poster child for the "learn as you go" approach to building a business.

In her early years, she spent nights in the Georgia Tech library researching patent law (she couldn't afford a lawyer, so she wrote her own patent, with help from a textbook from Barnes & Noble).

She spent weekends driving the five and a half hours to North Carolina, knocking on the doors of hosiery mills, begging them to manufacture her product.

She was determined to make Spanx a household name.

The rest, as they say, is history, and in March of 2012, Sara was named the world's youngest self-made female billionaire by *Forbes* magazine and one of *Time*'s 100 Most Influential People.

> Believe in your idea, trust your instincts, and don't be afraid to fail. It took me two years from the time I had the idea for Spanx until the time I had a product in hand ready to sell into stores. I must have heard the word "no" a thousand times. If you believe in your idea 100 percent, don't let anyone stop you!
> —Sara Blakely

Sara Blakely's story shows us the power of "winging it," trusting your path, standing strong, and learning as you go.

## Embrace the Lesson: Learn as You Go [3 Steps]

Step One: Identify the First Step

Moving forward doesn't mean you need to know everything; it just means you need to know the FIRST thing. Identify what your first step is: what is the first thing you can do to get the ball rolling? Whether it's buying a domain name, hiring a coach, starting a new Instagram accoun, or even simply figuring out your first step, DO IT!

Step Two: Take Action

Stop thinking about it and move into action mode. When you learn as you go, the only way to learn is to actually GO. Expect that you'll run into roadblocks and hurdles along the way but view these as an opportunity to learn and grow as you're taking massive action toward your big dreams and goals.

Step Three: Trust the Process

This is where you've gotta have a little faith in yourself! Trust that everything will happen and unfold exactly like it should. Give yourself grace, don't be too hard on yourself, and take advantage of all learning opportunities as you go along. You are capable of wondrous things!

# She Create[d] the Way

**Amber Dee**

Amber Dee and is an online business and digital marketing strategist. Her calling is to help entrepreneurs, brands, and creatives who want to attract their audience in less time.

Unlike a lot of others in her space, Amber has a master's degree in human behavior and is a licensed counselor, which gives her an edge to help her audience reach their target markets faster by understanding what attracts them and what sells.

Amber knew that the traditional path wasn't for her right after graduating with her undergrad degree.

She knew that her talents extended beyond the job she was hired to do, but she was terrified to branch out do her own thing . . . especially since she had just graduated.

But she was feeling stagnant at her job and knew there must be a bigger and better path out there for her:

> The job I had was just that, just a job. It limited my skills and my passion as well as my income.

It wasn't until I finished my master's degree that I felt more comfortable and confident to finally venture out.

I'm so glad I finally built up the confidence to pursue my own passions . . . my life is SO different now!

I have FREEDOM now. Freedom to make my own schedule and actually do the things I love. Being an entrepreneur has opened so many doors for me and allowed me to connect with so many people that I would have never met before.

Amber gets so much pleasure out of helping other female entrepreneurs achieve their own business goals.

When asked what tip or strategy she'd give to someone who wants to build an online business, without hesitation, she replies as follows:

Oh goodness! Hands down, consistency is the number one thing that will help you have a successful business. Other things you can do to have a successful business are collaborate and connect with other like-minded individuals. By yourself, you can grow . . . but with a crew, you can grow further.

Lastly, I recommend focusing your efforts. Don't try to do all the things at once. Find one or two things you can do best and be the expert there before you try to add on. Sometimes less really is more.

# CHAPTER 5

## make failure your BFF

What if you've been looking at failure the wrong way?

We're taught in life and in business that failure is a bad thing. It's a lack of success. An embarrassing collapse. A total defeat. A flop. *Right?*

Dead wrong.

Because not only is failure unavoidable, but also it's a natural part of your pathway to entrepreneurship.

If you want to be successful, it's time to embrace failure.

Creating your own path starts with making failure your BFF. And the sooner you can embrace the power of failing, the quicker you can move forward to bigger and better things.

So many of us use the fear of failure as an excuse to not succeed.

We remain stagnant, trapped in our current situations, simply because we're too afraid to move forward and risk not reaching our big dreams and goals.

But what if you could view failure not as rejection . . . but as redirection?

## Failure Is Redirection

Here's what's great about failure: it's an instinctive indication to redirect somewhere else.

Contrary to popular belief, failure is not a bad thing. Rather, it's a learning lesson to either pivot to a different direction, adopt a new approach, or move on completely.

I know what it's like to face entrepreneurial failure. In late 2015, after nearly two years as a full-time food blogger and wellness coach, I was forced to confront the reality that my current business had crumbled.

It was a reality that was months in the making. Of course, looking back, it's easy to see why it didn't work out: not the right structure or support in place and a lack of diversifying my income. But truthfully, the spark that I once had for my food blog and wellness business had dwindled away in the same direction as my business profits (a.k.a. downward into a pile of nothingness).

Even with that said, it was still an extremely emotional time for me. I had many sleepless nights, random cryfests, and feelings of self-pity and disappointment. If you've gone through something similar, you know the rollercoaster of emotions that comes along with it.

SHE CREATES THE WAY

In the midst of it all, I questioned everything and even regretted getting into entrepreneurship in the first place.

In fact, when I first went back to work (in my "dream job" as detailed in chapter 1), I vowed to say goodbye to being an entrepreneur for good.

Of course, looking back, failure became one of my biggest blessings in disguise.

It was that exact failure that acted as a pivot toward something that I realized was my true purpose in life: to show other females how to quit the job they hate and build a business they love.

I'm so grateful that first entrepreneurial endeavor didn't work out.

I can thank my failure for eventually leading me to my current successes, including launching what would become my fastest-growing business endeavor ever, the subscription box SHEclub Monthly; coaching and mentoring incredible clients; and, of course, writing this book!

## Two Reasons Why Failure Is Your Best Friend

Failure can be a serious ally to your big goals and aspirations. Here's why:

1. She reminds you how strong you are.

It's true that going through failure may feel like hitting rock bottom . . . I've been there, and I certainly had days where I didn't want to leave the safety of my bed (with Netflix on repeat and ice cream and wine on the bedside table).

But once you go through a failure or two and move past it, you're reminded how strong you are mentally and emotionally. Everything you built was pulled out from under you, and you're still here, ready to make your move.

It's kind of like your first love (and first breakup): while it's devastatingly crushing the first time around, after you come out the other side, you realize how strong and capable you are (and the next one is never as difficult to go through as the first).

2. She gives you advice.

The best BFFs not only listen to your hopes and dreams, but they also provide suggestions and help guide you toward the next step to take.

Failure is no different. She acts as a compass, redirecting you toward where you should go. She serves as a learning lesson to experiment and try new things in your business and life.

**Five Famous Females Who Overcame Failure**

Don't yet believe that failure is a necessary part of success? Here are five big examples of powerhouse women who overcame early struggles and business failures to achieve millions (and billions) in their life and business.

Arianna Huffington

She is one of the biggest names in the publishing world and the co-founder of *The Huffington Post*. But before launching *The Huffington Post*, Arianna Huffington had a very difficult time getting people to read her work. Her second book was rejected by thirty-six publishers. (Yes, you read that correctly—thirty-six!). Ariana kept going and often said that she was inspired and motivated by her mother's saying: "Failure is not the opposite of success . . . but a stepping stone to success."

Vera Wang

Vera Wang is a world-renowned fashion designer, but she wasn't always known for her high-end wedding gowns. In fact, she was once a figure skater, but she failed to make the US Olympic figure-skating team. She then moved on to work for *Vogue*, but was turned down for the editor-in-chief position before leaving to become a designer.

Ruth Fertel

Ruth Fertel is the founder of Ruth's Chris Steak House and recipient of the National Entrepreneur of the Year Award. She remortgaged her house to purchase her first restaurant, but it experienced huge losses due to frequent power outages. Later, a fire incident brought the entire restaurant down. Ruth was not discouraged and reopened another restaurant with the vision and tenacity to make it a success (and the rest, as they say . . . is history).

Oprah Winfrey

Hailed as the "Queen of Daytime Talk TV," Oprah Winfrey spent the initial six years of her life in poverty, living with her grandmother. At the age of nine, she was sexually attacked. At the age of fourteen, she got pregnant (and ultimately lost the baby). As an adult, Oprah was fired from her news reporter gig at a Baltimore news station. She then went on to build a successful following from her daytime talk show and production company. Oprah's net worth is currently valued at nearly $3 billion.

J.K. Rowling

She has sold over four hundred million books in her Harry Potter series . . . but what most probably don't know about J.K. Rowling was that she got fired from her job as a secretary before she hit it big. Back then, she was already dreaming of the foundations of Harry Potter in her mind. But all that daydreaming led to her getting fired, which then gave her the time to make her Harry Potter dreams a reality. She was a single mother on welfare when her first book was published.

**Embrace the Lesson: Make Failure Your BFF
[3 Journal Questions]**

If you've experienced a failure that you can't move past, it's time to reframe the situation as a learning lesson. Use these journal questions to embrace failure as part of your pathway to greatness.

Question One: What did I learn from the situation?

Question Two: How can I grow as a person from the experience?

Question Three: What are three positive things about the situation that I can take away?

# CHAPTER 6

## be courageous

The email replies were hitting my inbox in rapid succession.

"No, sorry, not interested."

"Thank you, but I will have to decline."

"Wish you the best, but it's not for me."

*Sigh.*

I took a long deep breath in, wondering if I actually wanted to move forward with this project.

It was late 2016, and even while working at my 9–5 job, I had decided to spearhead one of my most ambitious undertakings yet: an online summit.

The idea was to gather a group of female influencers and experts to interview about one of my current favorite social media platforms: Instagram. I would be the host, asking them questions on the topic as they shared their own personal tips and secrets for growth. Then the sessions would be presented in a free online summit, where attendees could tune in from anywhere across the globe.

I was so excited about this summit. But all of my excitement quickly came to a screeching halt when I realized I had one big problem: actually getting people to say YES to being featured in the summit.

I assumed it would be easy . . . I'd ask, and they'd reply with, "Of course! Can't wait!"

Unfortunately, I was finding that every person I asked either responded by politely declining, or worse, not replying at all.

I stared blankly at my computer screen, feeling deflated. The enthusiasm I once had was starting to dwindle away. I was becoming scared of approaching more people, for fear of being turned down yet again.

How many times have you had an idea and then abandoned it when it became difficult?

Maybe it was something small . . . you started to create a blog for your business, but encountered a small technical hurdle, so you made the decision to throw in the towel and ditch the blog completely.

Or perhaps you started writing your book but had such big writer's block on chapter 2 that you powered down your laptop and told yourself that maybe you'd get back to your book writing "next month."

Or maybe you made the conscious effort to start posting on social media more, but after a few negative comments from a faceless online Negative Nancy, you told yourself that perhaps social media just wasn't for you.

Here's the thing about stepping forward into bigger and better things: it takes courage.

It takes courage to look at your current situation and know that you're destined for more. To go to your 9–5 job every day, clock in and out, and know with everything within you that this will not be your truth forever . . . that this is just temporary.

But in order to make this a reality, you must be COURAGEOUS.

With courage comes bravery and strength to overcome any bump or blip in your entrepreneurial road.

Small technical hurdle? You'll learn about it and squash it.

Writer's block? You'll push through it.

Online Negative Nancy? You'll get over it.

> All of our dreams can come true if we have the courage to pursue them.
> —Walt Disney

**Courage = Vision**

Being courageous doesn't mean having an unrealistic outlook.

True courage is maintaining a vision, no matter what.

When you're courageous, it means you are keeping your vision strong with the unwavering belief that there's a better outcome at the end, despite moments of uncertainty.

Being courageous means stepping up even when you want to retreat back into a place of comfort.

After I caught myself wanting to pull back from my plans to put on the summit, I was reminded of my vision. A vision to host an online event that would ultimately impact thousands.

I knew I needed to remain brave, especially when facing the big pile of no thank-yous.

So, I pushed on, and every time I hit Send, I kept my internal vision alive and told myself that I would make this happen, no matter what. Even if it took sending one hundred requests for every yes I got in return, I kept my head held high with courage and pushed on.

And then, something happened: the tides started to turn. It wasn't just replies with polite declines; I was actually starting to get a few girls onboard with the project.

My big turning point came when Lauryn Evarts Bosstick, creator of *The Skinny Confidential*, sent me a message that she'd "be honored to be in the summit." Lauryn was a blogger whom I'd followed for years. She had grown her blog into a wildly successful brand that included a published book, a podcast, and had amassed millions(!) of followers across her website and social media platforms.

In all honesty, I had originally emailed her on a complete whim after meeting a few friends for happy hour (liquid courage?), fully convincing myself that there'd be no way she'd even reply, much less say yes.

When her reply popped into my inbox, my mouth gaped open. For me, this was like a celebrity joining my project. I was shocked, nervous, and a million times more excited than I was just a second prior. I called up one of my business besties and shared the good news.

"Can you believe it?" I squealed into the phone to my biz bestie, Kelli. "Can you believe that she said yes to ME? To little ole me?!? Jessica, toiling away at a cubicle during the day and building an online biz at night . . . while SHE is probably replying to me while she's got a glass of champagne in hand and vacationing in Bali or Greece or Bora Bora or something."

"Well of course she said yes to you!" Kelli replied encouragingly. "But she wasn't just saying yes to you, Jess . . . she believes in your vision for the summit!"

I smiled. Ah yes, the vision. It was my vision for the summit that ultimately gave me the courage to see the project through to completion.

I found myself using courage at every step of the summit: approaching big-name women to complete the speaker list, remaining confident while conducting the interviews, editing and presenting the content, and of course, putting it out into the world.

In the end, the summit was a huge success with over three thousand attendees. But most importantly, the entire experience acted as a reminder of how crucial it is to exude courage in our entrepreneurial endeavors.

Believe in every possibility (even the far-fetched ones, like your super-famous blog idol saying yes to your passion project).

Stand tall in your vision.

Most importantly, be courageous in all that you do.

**Embrace the Lesson: Be Courageous**
**[3 Steps]**

Step One: Exercise Your Courage Muscle

Just like focus and resilience, courage is a muscle.

You never know how strong you are until you are faced with the impossible. The more you flex your courage, the stronger it becomes.

Step Two: Hold the Vision

Keep your eye on the end goal in mind. Remind yourself of the positive impact you will make. It's the constant reminder of this vision that will provide you the courage you need during uncertain times.

Step Three: Trust the Process

Have faith that the "downs" you encounter will also come with "ups" and that everything happens for a reason. Be brave and confident that everything will fall into place the way it should. Remember, being courageous means stepping up even when you want to retreat back into a place of comfort.

# She Create[d] the Way

**Melissa Eckman**

Melissa Eckman is the creator of MelisFit, the #yogspiration movement, and a leader in the health, yoga, and beauty space with an online reach of over a million people worldwide.

Back in her corporate life, Melissa dedicated six years to building a profession in accounting. She always knew she was destined for more beyond her current circumstances but wasn't quite sure how she was going to get there.

Even with her hesitations, she made the brave decision to take the leap and pursue her true passions in health, yoga, fitness, blogging, and modeling. Melissa says:

> If I'm being totally honest with you ... I didn't know the plan (or what I was going to end up doing). I had my small personal blog @MelisFit_, my new yoga page @yogspiration, and small savings in my bank account to start a new life.

> I had no idea what my career was going to be, and quite honestly, was a little embarrassed that in my late twenties I was hitting the reset button on my life. All I knew is that I was following my heart, leading with my passion,

and hoping to make all my dreams come true.

Every step of the way people haven't believed in me.

People told me I wasn't good enough and made me feel they were better than me and just flat out wanted me to fail. A small part of me has always wanted to let those people win, and I would start to believe them and just want to give up because I thought, "Maybe they're right."

But if I would've done that...

I never would have gotten my first great accounting job out of college,
I never would have taken on teaching exercise classes while working sixty-five hours a week,
I never would have had the courage to start my blog,
I never would have been brave enough to leave my life of ten years in Florida to move to a new city,
I never would have signed with my modeling agency,
I never would have traveled the world,
I never would have made a career out of something I truly love,

I never would have fallen in love . . . and I wouldn't be the woman standing in front of you today.

Melissa has a strong message to other women who are dealing with negativity or judgment: stay focused on yourself. She says:

To anyone out there who is always made to feel less . . . the only person in life you have to answer to is yourself. Don't let ANYONE get in the way of happiness, following your dreams, or living the life you want to.

The only way you can ever fail in life is by sitting on the sidelines of your life because you're scared to go for it!

Make this next week your best week yet, and you can make all of your dreams come true.

# CHAPTER 7

# persevere, no matter what!

If you're truly ready to step away from the safe zone of being an employee, there's one important attribute that will make or break your entrepreneurial endeavors: perseverance.

You have to be willing to persevere, no matter what.

And just like courage will give you the strength, perseverance will provide the tenacity for you to keep going.

Here's what's so exciting about your next chapter: you're writing it. But the truth is that you don't truly know what the future holds.

If you're committed to persevering, you're planting your flag in the sand and making your statement to never, ever, ever give up.

Through the fear and the failures, with perseverance, you're armed with the tenacity to keep going.

Entrepreneurship is a roller coaster, and by having perseverance, you're strapping your seatbelt on for the crazy ride ahead. Because things WILL get crazy and messy (and everything in between) . . . not if, but when.

**When Things Get Messy**

What will you do when things don't go as planned?

It can be especially difficult to deal with the intricacies of business obstacles in our current online social and digital world. When we're all so interconnected, we feel even more exposed to the personal and entrepreneurial hurdles we encounter.

Perseverance is especially crucial when things get messy and we feel like we're embarrassingly exposed to the whole world.

When I was in ninth grade, like most new high schoolers, I just wanted to fit in. I didn't want to stand out; I simply wanted to blend in with the rest of the crowd.

So, I did what most teenagers do: I did what everyone else was doing. I bought the same Converse sneakers my friends had, watched the TV shows everyone else was talking about, and carried the same Trapper Keeper binder the other students carried around.

It was all about getting through high school while fitting in with the rest of the crowd (and with the least amount of embarrassing attention).

One November afternoon, just as my best friend Jeannie and I were exiting our sixth period class, it started pouring rain. It was a serious downpour, and the water was coming down so fast that it felt like the skies had opened up and someone had overturned a gigantic bucket of water over the high school grounds.

Normally, Jeannie and I would walk home after school together, side by side for the 1.3-mile walk back to our neighborhood. But given the drenched conditions on this particular day, there's no way we were going to WALK home.

Jeannie looked up at the sky, squinting her eyes shut as droplets of water hit her face. Then, her eyes popped open, and she looked at me with the I've-got-a-great-idea face . . .

"Hey," Jeannie said, "let's just hitch a ride with my older sister today. She just got her car!"

Jeannie's sister Andrea had recently turned sixteen and passed her driver's license test. She was the first person I knew at the school that got her license, and I was relieved to have an option to escape the rain and the twenty-five-minute drenched walk that I would inevitably have had to face.

"C'mon, we gotta hurry," Jeannie said. "She's probably on her way out to her car in the lot right now! We gotta run if we want to catch her."

I swung my red JanSport backpack across my back and took a deep breath while envisioning the quick run through campus that we were about to make. We'd have to take a sharp left at the restrooms, head through the asphalt quad, jump over the guardrails by the cafeteria, then run up and down the big grass hill at the parking lot entrance.

"Okay . . . let's do it," I replied, glancing toward Jeannie with a determined look.

"Ready?" Jeannie asked. I nodded. "Three, two, one . . . let's go!"

I sprinted forward, making a sharp left when I got close to the restroom, ran down through the quad, and hopped over the waist-high metal guardrails next to the cafeteria. Water dripped down my face, and I wiped across my eyes as I got close to the big grass hill at the parking lot entrance.

I looked around . . . it felt like EVERYONE was here. There was a line of cars waiting to pull into the parking lot, and hordes of students standing around, waiting for a ride home. It was like a sea of umbrellas, with teenage eyes peeking out from underneath, panning the scene as they looked for the right car.

"C'mon!" Jeannie yelled. "We won't be able to see her in the lot unless we get over the hill."

I bolted up the hill. It was a lot less solid than I remembered it. The rain had soaked through the grass, causing the mud to slide underneath my feet as I made my way up.

I was running at full speed when I reached the top of the hill, and when I went to descend down the grassy knoll, I started to lose my footing. Before I knew it, as I tried to move forward, I fell backward into a full-blown slide down the hill.

I lost complete control.

My arms flailed around, trying to grasp onto something while I slid down the wet, muddy, rain-soaked mound of dirt. I could feel the drenched dirt start to creep into the back of my jeans as I uncontrollably slid further and further.

When I reached the bottom, I turned around toward Jeannie, who had stopped dead in her tracks at the middle of the hill, mouth gaping.

"Uh . . . uh . . . Jessica?!? Are you okay?!?" she yelled out.

I glanced past Jeannie . . . toward the crowds of waiting, staring students, all eyes looking directly at me in my mud-soaked mess. They had seen it. They had witnessed it all.

My entire backside, rain-soaked mudslide had been watched by (what felt like) the entire student body of my high school.

I started crying. Uncontrollably. As the rain poured over me, matting my drenched hair to my cheeks and further permeating my brown-and-green mud-soaked jeans, the tears ran down and I buried my face in my hands.

I was extremely embarrassed. I just wanted to erase myself from the entire situation.

Fortunately, Jeannie spotted her sister. But unfortunately, after taking one look at my current state, Andrea stated that a ride home just wasn't possible.

"Are you kidding?!" Andrea squealed. "I literally just got this car. Like, last week. There is absolutely no way you're getting anywhere close to my car with all that mud on you."

I looked at Jeannie like a lost puppy just wanting to find a way home.

"Sorry," Jeannie said with a concerned tone. "You gotta walk home alone, Jess. It'll be alright . . ."

I knew what was next, even though I didn't want to do it.

I knew I would have to walk by the crowds of teenagers as they cracked jokes about my head-to-toe mud-soaked outfit. I knew I would have to walk the entire 1.3 miles back home as random cars and fellow students silently judged my embarrassingly disheveled appearance.

*What will YOU do when things get messy in your business?*

What will you do when all eyes are on you and everyone's watching?

Will you be able to trek through the mud to get to a better place?

There will be setbacks. There will be unexpected things that come up. There will be embarrassing, messy situations to get through.

By choosing the entrepreneur path, you're not just making the choice to own your own business . . . you're committing to taking everything head on and overcoming it, despite how surprising, difficult, or embarrassing it is.

Perseverance provides the assurance that you will get to where you want to go, no matter the rain, dirt, or muck that may be in your way.

When you persevere, you commit to getting through the mess, no matter what.

And you know what? I'm going to go out on a little bit of a limb here, but I'd like to tell you that if you've reached this far in the book . . . I already know that you possess the strength needed to persevere and succeed.

Girl, it's time to create your way with entrepreneurship.

And at the end of the day, it's not just about big ideas or dreams and hopes. It's about having the discipline to see it through. Quite simply, it's about being the last one standing.

You have the power to persevere and see all of your dreams come true.

Ready to make it all happen?

**Embrace the Lesson: Persevere, No Matter What!**
**[Visualization Prompt]**

Take a moment for yourself to participate in a personal visualization. I want you to imagine a time when you encountered something really challenging. Perhaps it was a scary large work task, a personal goal, a business hurdle, or a family issue. No matter the circumstances, remind yourself of how you felt as you began the process of working through it.

Now think of how you felt when you made it through to the other side. Undoubtedly, you were stronger and more powerful for having gone through the experience. Feel that power deep within you and reassure yourself that if you can get through that, you can through anything.

Mantra to repeat: *I will continue to move forward, no matter what. Nothing can stop me!*

# PART TWO

## create your way

# CHAPTER 8

# don't quit your day job... yet (hello, side hustle!)

Let's take a moment and say an extra special cheers to YOU, shall we?

If you're reading this, it means you're more than halfway through this book. But more importantly, you're making the crucial next step from embracing life's lessons to learning the actionable steps to creating the path to get there.

I hope at this moment you're feeling inspired and already envisioning the day you walk into your boss's office and submit your resignation letter, saying buh-bye to the traditional path and hello to the exciting world of full-time entrepreneurship.

But can I give you a little cautionary advice first? **Don't quit your day job . . . *YET*.**

Because even if your first thought when you woke up today was, "I'd rather walk on nails than walk into that cubicle today" (I've been there, girl), there's one big reason why keeping your 9–5 while you build your business is a smart move: STABILITY.

This is why the next portion of this book is geared for the woman who is side hustling. Because when you start and build your online business as a side hustle, your day job provides that critical stability.

Keeping your 9–5 while you grow your business helps you ride out the up-and-down roller-coaster waves of entrepreneurship that are inevitable.

I'm not saying you've got to stay at that job forever. In fact, we'll talk more about when it's the "right time" to put in your two weeks' notice.

But just know that it's important to keep your day job long enough to get past those first few big upside-down loops. After that, it's your call when you take the leap. And from there, the sky's the limit.

So buckle up, because we're rolling right into the three crucial components for turning your side hustle into full-time solopreneur success: time, monetizing, and expansion.

### Create Your Way: Don't Quit Your Day Job . . . Yet [Take Action]

Since it's probably not yet realistic to up and quit your 9-5 this very second, it's time to do the next best thing: put it on the calendar.

Whip out your planner, desktop calendar, iCal or Google Calendar, and scroll through the upcoming months to start thinking about your goal of when you'll take this side hustle to full-time. Then, pick a date. *An actual date.* And write "The Big Day!" on that exact date.

Make a promise to yourself that you'll use every last second between now and then to work your bootie off to make it happen (because you will!), while leveraging the stability that your corporate gig gives as you ride the entrepreneur roller coaster. You got this!

# She Create[d] the Way

## Cara Alwill Leyba

Cara Alwill Leyba is a best-selling author and master life coach who encourages women to live their most effervescent lives, celebrate themselves every day, and make their happiness a priority. She has over 2.5 million listeners worldwide tune in to her podcast, *Style Your Mind*, each week for powerful conversations and a megadose of inspiration.

In episode three of *Style Your Mind*, Cara shares how she left her full-time job to pursue her passions.

> I started my corporate career at *J Records*. It was my first real corporate job, and I had always wanted to work in the music industry. My dream was always to be a writer. I wanted to be a music journalist and to write for *Rolling Stone* or *Spin* or something like that.

> So I took this job at *J Records* and I was a receptionist, because I literally was like, just give me any job. I'll sweep the fricking floors. I don't even care. I just want to work for a record label.

> I was working as a receptionist at the front desk, and then at night I would go and assist the assistant to music mogul Clive Davis.

Cara learned so much from that administrative job, but she couldn't shake her burning desire to work directly in music. So she eventually left and scored a dream gig at MTV.

"I was making a lot of money, and I was building a team and getting promoted," she said.

But after a while, even while working at a powerhouse company like MTV with a great salary, she realized she was feeling stagnant and stuck.

> I suddenly found myself at a place where I thought . . . this is not what I thought it was going to look like. This is not inspiring. This is not creative. This is just not me. It's not who I am.
>
> Before you know it, seven years later, here I am in this job that I've been promoted now so many times. I'm a director at this point. I've got a big office. I've got a staff of nearly twenty people under me, and I felt like there was no way out. I felt totally trapped.

During her time at MTV, Cara had been blogging on the side at her blog *The Champagne Diet*, where she gives life advice and tips. She knew she needed to make a change in her own life, but wasn't quite ready to completely leave corporate without a safety net. So she got creative.

MTV offered tuition assistance to employees who wanted to take courses that would enhance their skills in their roles at the company. Cara, using her creativity, was able to convince her employer to pay for her life coaching education.

She explains, "I always suggest to people like be really creative about your current role. If you're not in a job that you love, but you want to move on to something that you do love, think about the skills you're acquiring and how you can put them into your next role."

After passing her life coaching course, she began taking on clients and building her life-coaching business as a side hustle:

> I'm charging along, I'm working, and I'm building the business and about another year goes by. I'm starting to pick up clients and starting to build streams of revenue. At that point, I had self-published a few books. Then I had come out with my third book, *Fearless & Fabulous*.

> That particular book was funny because it's all about fearlessness, and living your best life without fear, and being authentic and getting rid of all of that anxiety in your life that holds you back. But in the back of my mind, I knew that I hadn't made that one fearless jump yet. And that big fearless jump was leaving MTV and pursuing my passion.

Cara realized she wasn't reaching her full potential in her job. One random Wednesday, after sitting mindlessly at her desk for hours, she picked up her things and decided to spend the rest of the afternoon at one of her favorite places, the Plaza Hotel Champagne Bar.

She spent the remainder of the day sipping champagne, writing in her journal, and soul-searching. She said, "Everything that was coming out and flowing out of me was just telling me the same thing . . . you've got to take a chance on yourself, you have to pull the trigger. You just have to do this."

After convincing her brother to come meet her at the bar so she could share her thoughts with him, he agreed with her—she had to take the leap. When Cara wavered, he made her a compromise. Okay, don't quit your day job yet, he told her. Instead, just take ten days off and come to Japan. He paid for her flight, knowing that she'd use any excuse to stay home in the comforts of NYC. That trip changed everything for her:

> As soon as I got there, I thought, "This is life. This is what life should be. Life is not sitting at a cubicle in a fluorescent-lit office, commuting for an hour and a half each way during rush hour every day. That's not who I want to be anymore."

> Ten days later, I came home from Japan. A few days after that, I walked into my boss's

office, and I resigned. And that was it. I gave my two weeks' notice, and I left my job at MTV. The rest is history.

My advice to you is to shake it up. To get ripped out of your comfort zone. If you can go to Japan, I highly suggest it. Tokyo is amazing. But try to go somewhere and take a trip. And if you can't take a trip and physically go somewhere else, just start doing different things. Take a class, you know, take a wild, crazy dance class you would have never have taken. Something wild, something fun, something exciting. Just do something that you would normally have said no to.

I think that's when life starts to change . . . when we start to say yes to the things we're so accustomed to saying no to.

# CHAPTER 9

# create the time to get it done

Have you ever heard the saying, "You have the same amount of hours in a day as Beyoncé"?

While I appreciate the sentiment behind this quote, the reality is that most of us don't have the extra resources that a pop-culture icon has access to: personal assistant, private chef, publicist, nanny, etc.

However, that doesn't mean you can't teach yourself to be more productive with the twenty-four hours that we've all been allotted.

Proper time management is perhaps the biggest hurdle that side-hustle entrepreneurs face. Because sometimes you feel like all of your waking hours are devoted to your 9–5 job, so where will you find the time to work on your business?

Here's the key: be intentional. You'd be amazed at how much you can get done in a short period of time. Especially if you're hell-bent on making your dream come to life (which you should be!).

Now let's channel your inner time-management goddess and create more out of your everyday.

**4 Steps to Creating More Time in Your (Already Busy) Schedule**

**Step One: Batch Your Pockets of Time**

I tell all side-hustle entrepreneurs to approach time in batches.

Start off by looking at your day and finding the *pockets*: one-hour increments that you can devote to business time. Let's be honest, you won't find a ton of pockets lying around. However, you CAN find time nearly every day to devote to your side hustle (download the Time Pocket Formula PDF at shecreatestheway.com).

One week has 168 hours. So if you work 40 hours a week, that's 128 hours left over for sleep, eating, errands, family and friends, and of course, side-hustle entrepreneurship and business building.

When I was building my business on the side, my best batches of time were midday, during my one-hour lunch break. I'd keep my laptop and journal in the car, and when the clock struck twelve noon, I'd rush out of the office and jet a mile down the road to a local coffee shop, where I'd be able to squeeze in a good forty-five minutes of focused work.

I also (grew to) love early mornings. Which brings me to number two . . .

## Step Two: Adopt a Morning Routine

I know, I know, you might *hate* mornings. Perhaps you hit snooze twelve times before getting up. And let me tell you that I know how you feel! I considered myself a night person all of my life . . . until I adopted a morning routine. But when I was working full time while building my dreams on the side, I slowly switched my schedule around to wake up at 5:00 a.m. every morning.

Early morning really is the best time to get stuff done. You're more focused, less distracted, and scientifically, your brain is most creative during the first four hours that you're awake.

If you wake up an hour earlier than you normally get up, that gives you a whole sixty minutes to write a blog post, work on a sales page, create a module for an online course, etc. Think one hour doesn't make a difference? If you only have an hour every day to devote to your side hustle, that's thirty hours per month . . . 365 hours a year. It really adds up!

I get asked all the time about what my personal morning routine was when I was working full-time while building my business, so here it is:

- 5:00 a.m.: Alarm goes off and it's off to the kitchen. Drink a tall glass of water and take a probiotic.

- 5:05 a.m.: Make coffee while stretching (or force myself to do one minute of jumping jacks if I'm especially sluggish).
- 5:15 a.m.: Five minutes writing in my journal to get my brain going (things I'm grateful for and to-do items for the day/week).
- 5:20 a.m.: Sixty minutes straight of focused business work.
- 6:20 a.m.: Start getting ready for work.
- 7:30 a.m.: Off to work. Listen to an inspirational podcast or audiobook during the drive to work to get my mind primed for positivity.

**Step Three: Single-Task Your Work**

Whoever started the whole multitasking movement was totally wrong. Multitasking is not the ideal way to approach work . . . in fact, it's been scientifically proven that the more tasks you put on your plate, the less stuff you actually get done!

By trying to do a lot at once, you end up completing nothing. Instead, your time is spent feeling overwhelmed, while trying to juggle too many things.

This is where single-tasking comes in. If you struggle with focus, you've got to start single-tasking.

Single-tasking involves only focusing on one thing at a time.

Here's how you can approach single-tasking: first, look at what you want to complete for the week. Then, after you batch your pockets of time, write down one thing for each pocket of time, leaving a few pockets for catch-up on tasks that may take more time than planned.

If you have ten pockets of time in a week (a.m. and midday, Monday–Friday), here's how you might plan out your single-tasking:

1. Schedule Instagram posts for the week.
2. Write blog post.
3. Finalize blog post & format to send in Mailchimp.
4. *Catch-up time, if needed.*
5. Update About Me section on website.
6. Write outline for new digital course.
7. Plan out dates for digital course creation.
8. *Catch up time, if needed.*
9. Start writing detailed outline for Module 1 of new digital course.
10. Plan and schedule for next week (BIG goal for next week: complete Module 1 of new digital course).

Do you see how the plan is to only do ONE task during each hour of time? If you were to try and complete all of these things at once, you might end up sitting on the couch, watching an episode of *Real Housewives* instead of getting something done, because you'd be so overwhelmed.

When you single-task your work, you're able to focus and be more productive with your time. Win-win!

**Step Four: Start Big, Work Small**

This step applies specifically to planning. You have big goals for your entrepreneurial journey— *and you should.*

All great endeavors start with a dream of big change. But when it comes to actually approaching your daily tasks, you've got to work small.

You may feel like you have no clue of how you're going to achieve the goals you have for yourself. That's why you've got to break it down, babe . . .

Goals ==> Projects ===> Tasks

Start first by writing out the *goals* for yourself.

Then, explore what *projects* you'll need to complete in order to reach those goals.

From there, break down the projects into *tasks*.

By starting big and working small, it's easier to not only cross items off of your to-do list, but also to break down your great dreams into an attainable system.

And once you've mastered the art of getting things done in your side hustle (while still juggling your full-time job), it's time to move on to the next exciting component to transforming your side hustle into solopreneur success: monetization.

**Create Your Way: Find the Time to Get It Done
[Take Action]**

First and foremost, identify your time pockets (download the Time Pocket PDF inside the free bonus bundle at shecreatestheway.com). Then, use your new knowledge on how to create more time.

By being more cognizant of time as a whole, you'll find yourself being more focused and productive with your precious side hustle hours.

# CHAPTER 10

# monetize your passion

Okay, so you're ready to make money. You go, girl!

I can't tell you how exciting it is to generate your first sale in your business. Whether it's the sale of a $3 candle or a $3,000 consulting package, this first sale officially moves you from the category of "wantrepreneur" to definitive and legitimate entrepreneur.

At this point in the book you may have a good idea of what you want to do to monetize. However, if you can't stop thinking to yourself, "What the heck am I supposed to do to make money beyond a regular job?!?" this chapter's for you.

The truth is, there are a plethora of options you can explore for what to do to start generating money as a side hustle. I'm sure you've heard of most of them: start driving with a ride-sharing company, fill out surveys, complete quick gigs for other people, etc.

While these options are good for a little short-term cash, they aren't a long-term solution for mapping out your dream business and life. That's why I want you to think BIGGER than that . . .

Because the best way to generate purposeful profits that light you up is to start and build a business that is based around your biggest asset: *your knowledge.*

You have a gift.

It's unique to you, and only you can share it with the world. That's why your business should be an extension of YOU.

If you're still scratching your head for ideas of what you can pursue as an entrepreneurial endeavor, here are a few questions to ask yourself to help get your creative juices flowing.

**Monetizing Your Passions: 7 Questions to Ask Yourself**

1. What is my favorite hobby?
2. What are people coming to me for advice on?
3. What's a topic I know a lot about and I can't stop talking about?
4. What am I most passionate about?
5. What business idea can I launch the fastest?
6. Which business idea am I most likely to stick with?
7. What business is going to make me happy?

Now that you have a better idea of what you're naturally good at and what excites you, it's time to channel that passion into a business venture that puts you at the center of it all.

## 9 Different Ways to Make Money Online *(Based Around You)*

### Sell Your Services

Selling your services is the easiest way to start monetizing yourself. Use what you know and offer it as a service. The key here is to focus on what you're instinctively good at, and then offer a service where you charge per hour or per project.

Really great at organization and administrative work? Find work as a virtual assistant.

Love social media? Market yourself as a social media coordinator.

Passionate about the latest fashion trends? Offer in-home closet makeovers or personal shopping trips.

Here are some other service-based business opportunities to ponder:

- Personal trainer
- Photographer
- Professional organizer
- Resume helper
- Wedding planner
- Web builder
- Graphic designer
- Personal chef
- Online tutor

The benefit of selling your services is that it allows you to build connections in your industry while growing your side income.

**Provide 1-on-1 Consulting/Coaching**

Consulting and coaching is the next level beyond selling your services. You're positioning yourself as the expert to guide others on the topic you specialize in.

Consultants and coaches can also charge a higher price than those who are simply selling a service, because you're not just completing the work for someone, you're also teaching them how they can implement it on their end. And in today's digital world, all of this can be done virtually, via phone, Skype, or video calls.

Here are some consultant/coach ideas:

- Beauty consultant
- Life coach
- Wellness coach
- Marketing consultant
- Dating coach
- Social media consultant
- Career coach
- Writing coach
- Family coach
- Fitness coach
- Finance consultant
- Business coach

- Confidence coach
- Public speaking consultant

## Offer Group Coaching Sessions

Well, hello there, leveraged profits! By bundling up your coaching into a group session, you can now leverage your time and make more money in the same period of time.

Normally charge $75 per hour for coaching? Offer a group coaching session to ten people . . . *now you're generating $750 in that same hour.*

What's the best way to deliver group coaching? In my experience, I prefer webinars using my webcam so that everyone watching still feels like they're getting personal face-to-face time with me.

## Sell a Direct Sales Physical Product

Selling a direct sales product was my first tiptoe into entrepreneurship. I launched my food blog showcasing healthy, plant-based recipes, and sold a physical product via a direct-sales company that was directly in line with this (nutritional products).

Direct sales is an easy way to start your own business because it's turnkey and ready to go and has proven to be a profitable endeavor for many side hustlers who are passionate about the products they're selling and are excited to build a team around them.

**Sell Digital Affiliate Products**

Selling online affiliate products is a simple way to generate revenue without having to put in the time to create your own product from scratch.

What does affiliate mean? It means that by you marketing a product, you make a commission off of any sale that comes through your special affiliate link.

Personally, I only have one rule when it comes to being an affiliate for something: I must've already tried it myself AND loved it. I would never suggest promoting something that you didn't benefit from. You don't want to take the risk of recommending a lackluster product to your audience. (It could backfire!)

When you can generate revenue from something you honestly endorse and you know that whoever buys it will get a big benefit from it because you've already tried and loved it, it's a true win-win.

**Create and Sell a Digital Workbook or eBook**

Creating your own things to sell that bring you passive income? Now things are starting to get really fun!

One of the best ways to monetize yourself is to package up your knowledge into a digital workbook or eBook. Then, after you've created and set everything up, all of your income is completely passive.

Yup, you might be at work, at the movies, or just sitting in the bathtub with a glass of red wine when a sale comes in from a digital product you create. Plus, because YOU created it, nearly 100 percent of the profit goes directly to you!

**Create and Sell a Digital Course or Program**

Creating your own digital courses or online programs is one of the best ways to create a scalable business. Just like a digital workbook or eBook, with a digital course or program, you are simply packaging up your knowledge and selling it in the form of digital education.

Sometimes I hear from women who worry perhaps there are already too many digital courses out there and the market may be saturated. And this is where I have to reassure you that no one has sold your exact course yet . . . because only YOU can create it.

*Only you have your knowledge and experience.*

There are people out there right now that need what you have to offer.

With a digital course you can charge a premium price, generate passive income, and truly help others out in the world that need your help.

**Create (or Source) and Sell a Physical Product**

Nearly anything that can be sold, can be sold online. There are countless marketplaces to sell your own products, with the three of the largest being Amazon, eBay, and Etsy.

Perhaps you already have a craft hobby that you'd like to transform into a revenue-generating business, like:

- Candles
- Jewelry
- Scarves
- Purses
- Phone cases
- Hair bows
- Bridal party gifts
- Pillows
- Coffee mugs

Or, perhaps you have an item that you're passionate about that you'd like to source and resell in an online marketplace.

Either way, there has never been a better time to sell online. Things like drop-shipping via Amazon (where your bulk product is sent to Amazon and they ship to each customer individually) and simplified seller dashboards have made creating/sourcing and selling physical products a fruitful business for many online entrepreneurs.

**Launch a Subscription Box Business**

I've saved the best for last, as I'm a big advocate for the subscription box industry and founding my subscription box,

SHEclub Monthly, has completely changed my business and life.

When I first launched SHEclub, I simply wanted a way to provide physical inspiration to my tribe in addition to online trainings and courses to help them in their side hustle. What began as a small idea quickly blossomed into a transformative business endeavor.

A subscription box business is an incredible way to build sustainable, recurring revenue, because subscribers renew every month, giving you predictable profits in your business. Plus, it allows you to make a deeper connection to your audience with box goodies curated specifically for them.

You can start a subscription box business with relatively low start-up costs: simply purchase your first set of box goodies (with a target goal in mind), and when you sell out your first box, every month thereafter is pre-paid via subscriber renewals.

No matter what you select as your mode of monetization, my biggest piece of advice is this: don't waver. Start now.

There are unlimited resources out there, no matter what path you decide to take. But the longer you wait, the more you delay the start of your entrepreneurial dreams.

So . . . what are you waiting for? Let's go out there and make some money, honey.

**Create Your Way: Monetize Your Passion**
**[Take Action]**

You're ready to get super-duper clear on your passions, so the next step is to identify your knowledge and passions then transform that into a monetizable offer. Whether it's a service, product, or something else, pick one and GO FOR IT.

To learn more about how to make your first $1,000 in your side hustle, check out the free webinar training at: jessica-debry.com/1kwebinar

# She Create[d] the Way

## Robyn Baldwin

Robyn Baldwin is the founder and creator of the *Alpha Female Podcast*. Her goal is to help inspire others to tackle the world head-on with positivity and enthusiasm while finding work/life harmony in a happy and healthy way.

Robyn is not just preaching about work/life harmony; she's LIVING it as a full-time ecommerce merchandising manager and also a blogger, podcaster, author, and essential oil educator.

She fell in love with building side hustles when she realized she was ready to monetize and diversify her income:

> I started blogging in 2009, podcasting and building a network marketing business in 2016, and I published a book in 2016 as well. The spark to truly monetize my passion in side hustles was when I was diagnosed with multiple sclerosis in 2014.
>
> I wanted to ensure that if there was ever a day that I might be fired (I don't intend there to be!), let go, or not capable of working in a full-time setting, I'd have a side hustle income that would be my safety zone.

Robyn admits that life at the current moment requires a lot of planning, but she's always been really good at that: "Being super organized and detail-oriented suits side hustle work very well. It's also more focused on 'business' and passion activities vs. escapism ones like partying or watching endless hours of TV. Although . . . I do have to admit I love a good Netflix binge every now and again!"

Like all entrepreneurs, Robyn's had her fair share of ups and downs, but she is proud of pushing through the tough times:

> Publishing *Love Lost, Life Found* in August 2016 was a super-proud moment. I took a tragedy, worked on healing myself, and then published not only my story but also my steps to healing a broken heart and finding a life that I now love.
>
> I'm also proud that I've grown my networking marketing business to the rank of Silver. It's a small token that reminds me I've had the amazing opportunity over the course of almost two years to really make an impact in the lives of a lot of people and teach about health care and self-care empowerment through simple tools like essential oils.

While the financial gain is coming, it's the relationships and impact that I'm making that fill me up more.

Robyn encourages newbie entrepreneurs to get clear on why they're starting their business in the first place. "Get really clear on your why," she states. "What is your intention behind it? Once that's locked and loaded and you have full belief in it, you will soar."

# CHAPTER 11

# expand your brand (and email list)

Now that you know how to manage your time and you've chosen how you're going to monetize your passions, it's time to talk about the one thing that will make or break your online business.

If you've tried to sell your products or services on social media in the past (with no success) and you're feeling a bit frustrated with what you should be spending your time on instead, here's your answer: your email list.

When you're growing an online business, you must also be growing your email list.

The fact is, people will buy from you because they know you, like you, and trust you. But HOW is this created online? *Connection and trust are built online through consistent communication.*

Building your email list is the most surefire way to have a sustainable, profitable business.

Statistics have shown that one email address is more impactful on your business than twenty social media fans.

Yup, that means that one hundred people on your email list is better than two thousand fans on social media!

I want to point something out: you can have the best services, coaching, and products out there AND be a master at getting stuff done, but if you don't have an audience and email list to sell to, it means nothing.

This is where I see a lot of side hustlers fall short. This is where they give up. They think that success isn't meant for them, when in reality, they haven't even attempted to build their email list yet.

Here's the thing: the majority of people who visit your website or store will never return. In addition, the chances of generating a sale on someone's first visit is very slim.

So what should you do instead?

Instead of driving traffic to a sales page, direct them to join your email list.

The goal is to capture their email address so you can continue to connect with them in the future and share content.

This is called *push marketing*, where you take your product to the consumer. It is the opposite of *pull marketing*, where you try to bring consumers to your product.

In other words, this is the difference between always trying to pull people over to your website/store (this is very hard to do!) vs. having an email list to push out your new blog posts, valuable content, and of course, what you're selling. With the power of push marketing, you can build connection and trust with the individuals on your email list, and ultimately, lead your audience to buy from you.

So say buh-bye to hearing crickets when releasing your offer on social media, and say HELLO to the payment notification DING (best sound ever!) when sharing your offer with your email list.

It's time to get out there and engage in activities that will help you expand your brand and your email list exponentially.

There's a lot of noise online on different ways to build your email list. I'm sure you've hear most of them: Run Facebook ads! Connect with others on Twitter! Start a group on LinkedIn! Pin everything on Pinterest! Etc., etc., etc.

While all of the aforementioned social media strategies DO work in building your email list when executed correctly, I thought it'd be more beneficial for you to learn a handful of methods that are a little bit different than the norm.

These email list tactics are a little out-of-the-box, but they work. Trust me. (I've used them all!)

**5 Ways to Grow Your Email List** *(That You Haven't Tried Yet!)*

**Write a Guest Post for a Big-Name Blog or Website**

When I work with new female entrepreneurs, they all ask me

the same question: "But how will people FIND me online? And how do I grow my email list?" And to that I reply, "Write a guest post!"

Here's why guest features are so great: because even if you are brand new, you can leverage their BIG following to get eyeballs (readers and potential future customers!) to see your stuff.

When I first started out in the entrepreneurial world with my food blog, just like every other newbie, I was a nobody. But then, I had a recipe posted on a popular wellness site called *MindBodyGreen*, and suddenly my email list grew by two hundred in less than twenty-four hours. (Hello, potential future customers!) That single experience opened my eyes to the power of guest posting . . . and the rest, as they say, is history.

## Be Interviewed as a Guest on a Podcast

Podcasts are all the rage right now, and it's easy to see why, as you can tune in and listen from nearly anywhere. Because of this, many new entrepreneurs see the potential in podcasting but aren't quite ready to launch their own podcast for their business and brand.

Enter podcast guesting, where instead of having to create, edit, and produce your own podcast episodes from scratch, you simply appear as the featured guest.

Being interviewed as a guest on a podcast gives you immense exposure in exchange for a very short investment of time. Not only that, but the interview allows you to tell your personal story and connection to your business, thus building trust and increasing likability with the listener.

Not sure how to go about being featured on a podcast? Here's the quick answer: do your research. Spend time looking at podcasts in your niche on your favorite podcasting app, then go a step further and do a little investigative work to find the host contact info. Drop them a line inquiring if they're looking for guests. You'd be surprised at how many are looking to book out their calendar and are open to interviewing YOU.

**Publish a Book on Amazon**

This is easier than you think—pinky promise. Amazon makes it super simple for self-publishers to sell their books on the Amazon platform.

Here's why I advocate for publishing a book on Amazon: because people use Amazon as a SEARCH ENGINE, searching for various things, just like Google.

The benefit to Amazon is that your books can live on there forever (unlike social media, where only the most recent content shows at the top). Publishing is also a great way to build credibility while expanding your brand (and to generate revenue in the process).

**Host an Online Giveaway**

Giveaways are so fun! And let's be honest, everyone loves the chance to win free stuff.

Here's a simple way to host an online giveaway: choose three to five products from Amazon, post about them on social media informing your audience that they must join your email list in order to be entered into the giveaway. When the winner is announced, order the products from Amazon to be shipped directly to the winning individual. That way, Amazon takes care of all the organizing/handling/shipping directly to the winner of the giveaway. Easy-peasy.

Pro tip: When planning your giveaway, link up with a few other side hustlers or female entrepreneurs so you can all leverage your audiences to work in conjunction with each other for more exposure.

**Host an Actionable Webinar**

Webinars are not only a great opportunity to share your knowledge and paint yourself as the expert in your field, but they are a fantastic way to grow your email list.

People buy from people that they know and trust, and webinars allow you build up the know-and-trust factor simply by you sharing actionable, valuable content.

The more webinars you host, the more people will attend each one. Word gets out fast. More attendees = bigger audience = bigger profits.

The key here is growth. You don't have to do everything, but pick one thing that will help you expand and build your brand. Then, be intentional and implement!

> ### Create Your Way: Expand Your Brand
> ### [Take Action]
>
> Making your business visible online is all about thinking outside the box. Using the suggestions in this chapter as a starting point, pinpoint what will be your avenue for expansion and exposure in the next stages of your business.
>
> As you move forward and increase your visibility in the digital space, always be promoting the place where the audience can join your email list. That way, you're not just increasing brand awareness, but growing your email list too - an invaluable asset for future profits.

# CHAPTER 12
# go basic:
# 10 steps to online success

Now that you understand the three crucial components for turning your side hustle into full-time solopreneur success, you might wonder how you reach entrepreneur success as quickly as possible.

The truth is, just like there's no magic pill for weight loss, there's no magic formula to big business achievements.

But I will say that entrepreneurs (especially us female entrepreneurs!) tend to overanalyze the process, thereby delaying action and movement forward. That's why I wanted to make sure to include this ten-step list . . . because it serves as a reminder to get back to the basics.

If you're overwhelmed with the bajillion things you think you need to do in order to reach success, and perhaps you feel like you're running around with no direction, it's time to step back.

Whether you haven't yet dipped your toe into entrepreneurship and you're just beginning to carve your path, or you're a more seasoned entrepreneur looking for guidance, these are the ten steps that can provide a loose framework for your incredible journey ahead:

**Step One: Find concept clarity in who you are and who you're really serving.**

If you're trying to help everyone, you end up helping no one. Getting clear on who you are, what your strengths are, who you're helping, and where you're going is the foundation of your business. (Refer back to the seven questions in chapter 10.)

Think about it: when you're searching online for help with something, your inquiry is pretty clear, right? Your future clients can only find YOU online if you narrow down your concept clarity.

**Step Two: Create a website that is a virtual embodiment of your concept clarity.**

Your website is your virtual storefront to the world, and visitors will make up their mind within ten seconds of being on the homepage whether or not they plan to stick around.

Creating a website that easily portrays what you do and who you can help is critical to attracting your audience, and essentially your perfect clients, to you.

**Step Three: Attract your perfect client with your lead magnet.**

Nowadays, in our busy sea of, "Join my email list!" it's

important to stand out from the crowd and offer a valuable bonus right from the start.

Your lead magnet can be anything that relates to your brand—a checklist, cheat sheet, mini-training, etc., whatever you know that will draw in an audience and appeal to your perfect client or customer.

**Step Four: Consistently grow an email list of adoring fans.**

Just like you learned in chapter 11, growing your email list is one of the best ways to secure a sustainable, profitable business online.

People will buy from you because they know you and like you—and that connection is built over time, via an email list, by providing steady, valuable content.

**Step Five: Build your online brand with consistent, valuable content.**

Here's where everything starts to work together. By growing your email list AND providing consistent content, it's a win-win: you keep your current list happy with new content, while continuing to attract others and grow your list.

By sharing your tips, stories, and expertise with the world, you're not only reaching countless others online, you're also building your brand with your awesome content.

**Step Six: Increase your web traffic and expand your audience online.**

It's not enough to have a great website with great content if no one can see it, right? It's like having a beautiful house with no visitors. What's the point?

Expanding online is like a farmer planting seeds: the more you plant, the greater your chance of success.

Step outside your comfort zone and do things that you haven't tried yet: film a video, be interviewed on a podcast, collab with another entrepreneur in your space, etc. You never know where your next paying client will find you. (Refer back to chapter 11 for more on this.)

**Step Seven: Create connection and trust in the virtual world using webinars.**

Yes, there's definitely a lot of hype around webinars. And it's because webinars WORK. There is no other platform that allows you to go from stranger to leader (in the eyes of the audience) in only sixty minutes flat.

Webinars are an incredibly powerful way to prove your expertise, provide valuable content, and sell your offerings to the world, all from the comfort of your home.

**Step Eight: Improve your social proof and connect with your audience via social media.**

Let's face it, we live in a "Google it" society, and everyone looks up everything nowadays. This includes your audience.

Whether or not you like it, your legitimacy is measured partially on your social media presence. It's not all about follower count, it's about providing fresh content on a regular basis that ties in directly with your brand, blog, business, and perfect client.

Feel overwhelmed with all the social media platforms out there? I recommend starting with only ONE and mastering it before moving onto the next.

**Step Nine: Launch a digital or physical product that your perfect client is dying to purchase.**

This is where your online business starts to get really fun. Because you're taking what your audience needs help with (a.k.a. what they'll pay money for), creating a solution, and packaging it all together into an irresistible product.

Whether it's a book, training, digital course, coaching package, subscription box, physical product, or something else, you can leverage your expertise to truly serve your tribe (refer back to chapter 10 for more on this).

**Step Ten: Rock your launch, rake in the profits, and live happily ever after. (This is just the beginning.)**

Don't just hope things will fall into place. Instead, create a launch strategy for your offering, map it out, sequence your marketing, and create a big BUZZ for what you have to sell.

With this approach, your audience will be knocking at your virtual door to buy . . . which means a bigger bank account, a bigger business, and, most importantly, a bigger sense of purpose.

# She Create[d] the Way

## Amy Porterfield

Amy Porterfield has been named by *Forbes* as one of the Top 50 Social Media Power Influencers. With a top-ranked business podcast, best-selling online courses, multiple seven-figure revenue streams, and 250,000+ loyal subscribers, it's obvious that Amy is a top-notch entrepreneur.

But it wasn't that long ago that Amy was devoting all of her time and energy into a corporation, leaving her with little to no time for her loved ones and true passions.

Amy has an incredible story in that she scored a dream gig working for Tony Robbins, but soon learned that she wanted to pave her own path. In episode 175 of her *Online Marketing Made Easy* podcast, she shares how she went from a corporate gal with a side hustle, to full-time entrepreneurship:

> I was asked to take notes at a meeting that Tony was doing with a bunch of internet marketers. I wasn't even at the main table. I was at a side table, and the guys that walked into the meeting were Frank Kern, Eben Pagan, Jeff Walker, and so many others (those are just a few that were at the table) and it was amazing.

Tony went around the table and asked them to tell him about their business. Each of the guys talked about their lifestyle, all the freedom they had, and the ability to create and try new things and launch this and that. The whole idea of an online launch was completely foreign to me, but it was one of those moments that my heart just started beating like crazy. "What are they talking about? I NEED that."

After that meeting I turned in my notes and did what I needed to do. But I thought I had to have a piece of that. I had to be a part of whatever the heck they were talking about. This is part of my secret to success, but what I did was figure out a way to get in there.

Amy states that she gets asked all the time why she would ever leave a well-paying, really exciting job with Tony Robbins. In her own words:

The answer to that, my turning point is that after all of those experiences of getting to work on online launches and taking notes in that one really cool meeting that kind of changed my life, I was bursting at the seams to be my own boss.

I wanted nothing more than to call the shots and to dictate my own hours and create the content I was most excited to create for my own business. Can I get an amen? I know that a lot of you are still in your 9-to-5 corporate job.

I bet you are getting close to that point that you are bursting at the seams. Here's the advice I want to give you ... You have to listen to your gut in this. I promise you there is never a perfect time to leave corporate.

Amy spent many months working on her business as a side hustle while still working for Tony.

She was growing her income on the side while still juggling her corporate work, waiting for the right time to come along before completely leaving and become a full-time entrepreneur.

She explains that you never feel totally comfortable when you leap:

I didn't want to get resentful. That wasn't fair for anybody. So I finally took the leap when things were not perfect, but I knew if I didn't do it now I may never do it.

I think you've just got to get to that point. I know a lot of moms say, 'You'll never find the perfect time to have a baby. There's never a perfect time.

She explains that Tony teaches a story around the need to burn the boats and storm the island when you finally make a really big decision and there's no turning back.

> For me, burning the boats meant I couldn't take any contractor work for Robbins.
>
> I couldn't go to one more event or do one more side job for them because I knew that was my safe spot. I would go right back into working for corporate again because I was so scared to go out on my own.
>
> You need to cut ties. You need to keep moving forward.

# CHAPTER 13

## *two weeks' notice*

Perhaps the most dreamt about time for any female entrepreneur is the day they get to present their two weeks' notice to their employer.

In other words, the day that you quit your 9-5 job and begin the journey into full-time entrepreneurship.

I remember daydreaming about this moment for months. I would ponder what would be in my resignation letter, the exact words I would say to my boss, and basically every last detail (even down to the outfit I would wear).

It is exciting and uplifting to imagine these details and to picture the day when it all happens.

However, in my real life and in full transparency, I never really felt 100% ready to make the transition.

Don't get me wrong, my side hustle was growing at a steady rate. In just fifteen months, while still juggling my full-time corporate job, I had accomplished a lot: I created and hosted an online summit with thousands of registrants, grew my email list by over 3,000, celebrated a $10K month (twice!), coached amazing women, and was in the very beginning pre-launch stages of SHEclub, my monthly subscription box.

But even with all of this, I was still terribly uncertain about the future and would lie awake at night wondering when the "right time" would actually happen.

The fact is, I wasn't yet making a steady income in my business that consistently surpassed my corporate salary. Furthermore, I was scared that I was doomed to repeat my first failure in entrepreneurship and I refused to go through all of that again.

So, I waited for the right time. And waited. And waited. And it never came.

I'm going to let you in on a little secret: *the right time doesn't exist.*

In fact, I'd argue that if the perfect time comes your way ... you waited too long. The reality is, at some point, you must trust yourself and trust the process.

I knew I was capable of taking my business to the next level. I also knew that I had done a helluva lot of work in my side hustle to make sure that this venture into entrepreneurship was going to be completely different than my previously failed one. That's why, after finally taking my own advice (and quite honestly, after a four-day immersion event with Tony Robbins), I realized that NOW was the ideal time to make the transition.

Instead of looking for the right or perfect time to submit your two weeks' notice, you should be looking for something else: *the ideal time.*

The ideal time isn't perfect. It's also not absolutely certain. But if you've done your homework, put in the time, and have been consistently taking action on your goals, you've already rode the harshest waves of entrepreneurship and set yourself up for success.

If you've implemented what you've learned thus far in this book, you're on the right path. You've embraced the life lessons, mastered your time, are already monetizing, and your business is growing and expanding at a steady pace. You're now seeing the fruits of your labor ... so when is your time to transition into full-time entrepreneurship?

If the perfect world existed, the right time would be crystal clear. You'd have passive income that far surpassed your paycheck, more customers and clients than hours in a day, and you'd be feeling completely confident about quitting your job (wouldn't that be nice?).

*But if you're waiting for the perfect time, you'll be waiting forever.*

**Don't wait for perfect; aim for ideal.**

In the real world, you'll never reach the exact right time.

However, after putting in months of dedication in your side hustle, you'll start to get the inkling that NOW is the ideal time. You'll feel nervous and excited all at once, with the giddiness that comes with knowing you're about to take a big step forward.

You don't need to have everything perfect. You just need to embrace the work you've done thus far and trust the path that you've created for yourself.

Then, it's your duty to walk down that path.

Find the ideal time and submit your two weeks' notice. You go, girl.

# CHAPTER 14

# write your own story

Now that you're nearly finished with this book, it's time to write your own story.

You are the author of your life . . . might as well make it a great one, filled with following your heart and going after your big dreams.

And you're ready for it. Now is your time to say buh-bye to a lackluster existence and hello to carving your own future.

Ditching the traditional path and creating your own way is terrifying, exhilarating, and amazingly gratifying all at the same time. But let me assure you that this will be the most incredible journey you'll ever embark on.

Entrepreneurship is truly an extraordinary way to make a living.

You are capable of so much. I believe in you.

I can't wait to see what your future holds.

she is destined for more.
she creates the way.

# RESOURCES

To access printable PDFs, inspirational wallpapers, and more downloads that correspond with this book, go to: www.shecreatestheway.com

To learn more about SHEclub Monthly, the first subscription box created specifically for side hustle entrepreneurs, go to: www.sheclubmonthly.com

To learn more about how to make your first $1,000 in your side hustle, go to: www.jessica-debry.com/1kwebinar

To learn more about how to start a subscription box business, go to: www.jessica-debry.com/subboxwebinar

To visit Jessica online, learn more about her story, read blog posts for side hustlers and online entrepreneurs, and find out more about her coaching, mentoring, and digital trainings, go to: www.jessica-debry.com

To find the woman who is powerful enough to say yes to her dreams and follow her heart, walk over to the nearest mirror and stare deep into the eyes of the person reflecting back at you. It's you. *It's always been you.*

# HIRE JESSICA TO SPEAK

Jessica DeBry is a dynamic and engaging leader who is well-versed in speaking at nearly any sized event: from small intimate gatherings of twelve women to large-scale events of 500+.

**Jessica's speaking topics include:**

- Making Failure Your BFF
- Morning Routine for Achievers
- Embracing the Struggle
- Side Hustle Strategy for Success
- The Recurring Revenue Model
- Overcoming Self-Sabotage
- And so much more!

Contact her directly at Jessica@Jessica-DeBry.com

# NOTES:

# NOTES:

# NOTES: